SACRED READING

for Advent and Christmas
2015–2016

SACRED READING

for Advent and Christmas
2015–2016

Apostleship of Prayer

Douglas Leonard, Executive Director

AVE MARIA PRESS AVE Notre Dame, Indiana

Excerpt from *Three Moments of the Day: Praying with the Heart of Jesus* by Christopher S. Collins, S.J. Copyright ©2014 by Wisconsin Province of the Society of Jesuits. Published by Ave Maria Press.

Founded in 1865, Ave Maria Press is a ministry of the United States Province of Holy Cross.

www.avemariapress.com

Paperback: ISBN-13 978-1-59471-609-6

E-book: ISBN-13 978-1-59471-610-2

Cover image © Thinkstock.

Cover and text design by David Scholtes.

Printed and bound in the United States of America.

CONTENTS

INTRODUCTION

Advent is all about waiting for Jesus Christ. The Gospel readings of Advent make us mindful of three ways we await Jesus—past, present, and future. First, we remember and accompany Mary, Joseph, and the newborn Jesus. Second, we prepare for the celebration of his birth this Christmas, so that the day doesn't pass us by with just meaningless words and worthless presents. Third, we anticipate the second coming of Jesus Christ, who will come in power and glory for everyone to see and establish his kingdom of peace and justice upon the earth.

Christ is born, and we follow him in exile and in those joyful early years with the Holy Family. We are blessed, but we are challenged, too, to understand the ways of God and how we personally may understand and respond to them now.

One of the ways we can better understand and respond to the Lord during this holy season of Advent is by rediscovering, along with Christians all over the world, a powerful, ancient form of prayer known as sacred reading (lectio divina). What better way to deepen one's friendship with Jesus Christ, the Word of God, than by prayerfully encountering him in the daily Gospel? This book will set you on a personal prayer journey with Jesus.

Sacred Reading takes up this ancient practice of lectio divina in order to help you to engage the words of the daily Gospel, guided by the Holy Spirit. As you read and pray this way, you may find—as many others have—that the Lord speaks to you in intimate and surprising ways. The reason for this is simple: as we open our hearts to Jesus, he opens his heart to us.

Saint Paul prays beautifully for his readers:

> For this reason I bow my knees before the Father, from whom every family in heaven and on earth takes its name. I pray that, according to the riches of his glory, he may grant that you may be strengthened in your inner being with power through his Spirit, and that Christ may dwell in your hearts through faith, as you are being rooted and grounded in love. I pray that you may have the power to comprehend, with all the saints, what is the breadth and length and height and depth, and to know the love of Christ that surpasses knowledge, so that you may be filled with all the fullness of God. (Eph 3:14–19)

How to Use This Book

This book will set you on a personal prayer journey with Jesus from Ash Wednesday through the end of Holy Week. Please note that some of the readings in this booklet have been shortened for group use. In each case the citation for the unabridged reading is marked with an asterisk (*), followed by a parenthetical citation that includes the verses in the booklet. *Sacred Reading: The 2016 Guide to Daily Prayer* contains the unabridged Gospel texts for the entire liturgical year, and is available online through the Apostleship of Prayer website, or through your local bookstore.

In prayerful reading of the daily Gospels, you join your prayers with those of believers all over the world.

Following the readings for each season of the liturgical calendar, you will be invited each day to reflect on
the Gospel text for the day in six simple but profound
steps:

*1. Know that God is present with you and ready to
converse.*

At all times God is everywhere, including where you
are in this very moment. The human mind is incapa-
ble of fully grasping the mystery of God, but we do
know some things about God from scripture. God is
the transcendent ground of all being, invisible, eternal,
and infinite in power. God is love, with infinite love
for you and me. God is one with and revealed through
the Word, Jesus Christ, who became flesh. Through
him all things were made, and by him and for him
all things subsist. Jesus is the way, the truth, and the
life. He says that those who know him also know his
Father. Through the passion, death, and resurrection
of Jesus, we are reconciled with God. If we believe in
Jesus Christ, we become the sons and daughters of
almighty God.

God gives us the Holy Spirit to lead us to truth and
understanding. The Holy Spirit also gives us power
to live obediently to the teachings of Jesus. The Holy
Spirit draws us to prayer and works in us as we pray.
No wonder we come into God's presence with gladness. All God's ways are good and beautiful. We can
get to know God better by encountering God in the
Word, Jesus himself.

The prompt prayer at the beginning of each day's
reading is just that—a prompt, something to get you
started. In fact, all the elements in the process of sacred

reading are meant to prompt you to your own conversations with God. After reading the prompt, feel free
to continue to pray in your own words: respond in
your own way, pray in your own way, and hear God
speaking to you personally. Your goal is to make sacred
reading your own prayer time each day.

2. *Read the Gospel.*

The entire Bible is the Word of God, but the Gospels
(Matthew, Mark, Luke, and John) specifically tell the
Good News about Jesus Christ. Throughout the Church
year, the daily Gospel readings during Mass will come
from all four Gospels. Sacred Reading concentrates on
praying with the daily Gospels. These readings contain
the story of Jesus' life, his teachings, his works, his
passion and death on the cross, his resurrection on the
third day, and his ascension into heaven.

The Gospels interpret Jesus' ministry for us. Much
more, by the Holy Spirit, we can find in the Gospels
the very person of Jesus Christ. Prayerful reading of
the daily Gospel is an opportunity to draw close to
the Lord—Father, Son, and Holy Spirit. As we pray
with the Gospels, we can be transformed by the grace
of God—enlightened, strengthened, and moved. Seek
to read the Gospel with a complete openness to what
God is saying to you. Many who pray with the Gospel
recommend rereading it several times.

3. *Notice what you think and feel as you read the Gospel.*

Sacred reading can involve every faculty—mind, heart,
emotions, soul, spirit, sensations, imagination, and

much more—though usually not all at once. Different passages touch different keys in us. Sometimes we may laugh. Sometimes we may need to stop and worship before we continue. Sometimes we will be puzzled, amazed, stung, abashed, reminded of something lovely, or reminded of something we had wanted to forget.

Seek to feel all of your emotions as you read. Apply your intellect, too. You will confront problems of context and exegesis on a daily basis. That's okay. Sometimes you may experience very little. That's okay, too. God is at work anyway. Give yourself to the Gospel and take from it what is there for you each day.

Most important, notice what in particular jumps out at you, whatever it may be. It may be a word, a phrase, a character, an image, a pattern, an emotion, a sensation—some arrow to your heart. Whatever it is, pay attention to it because the Holy Spirit is using it to accomplish something in you.

Sometimes a particular Gospel repeats during the liturgical year of the Church. To pray through the same Gospel even on successive days presents no problem whatsoever to your sacred reading. Saint Ignatius of Loyola, founder of the Jesuits and author of *The Spiritual Exercises*, actually recommends repeated meditation on passages of scripture. Read in the Spirit, Gospel passages have unlimited potential to reveal to us the truths we are ready to receive. For the receptive soul, the Word of God has boundless power to illuminate and transform the prayerful believer.

4. *Pray as you are led for yourself and others.*

Praying is just talking with God. Believe God hears you. Believe God will answer you. Believe God knows what you need even before you ask. Jesus says so in the Gospel. So your conversation with God can go far beyond asking for things. You may thank, praise, worship, rejoice, mourn, explain, question, reveal your fears, seek understanding, or ask forgiveness. Your conversation with God has no limits. God is the ideal conversationalist. God wants to spend much time with you.

Being human, we can't help being self-absorbed, but praying is not just about our own needs. We are often moved by the Gospel to pray for others. Often we will remember our loved ones in prayer. Sometimes we will be led to pray for someone who has hurt us. At other times we will be moved to pray for a class of people in need wherever they are in the world, such as for persecuted Christians, refugees, the mentally ill, teachers, the unborn, or the lonely.

We may also pray with the universal Church by praying for the pope's prayer intentions. Those intentions are entrusted to the Apostleship of Prayer and are available through its website and its annual and monthly leaflets. You may get your own copy of this year's papal prayer intentions by contacting the Apostleship of Prayer. The Apostleship is known as the pope's prayer group, and has more than fifty million members worldwide. Jesus asked us to unite in prayer, promising that the Father would grant us whatever we ask for in his name.

5. Listen to Jesus.

Jesus the Good Shepherd speaks to his own sheep, who hear his voice (see Jn 10:27). This listening is a most wonderful time in your sacred reading prayer experience. The italicized words in this passage are the words I felt impressed upon my heart as I prayed with these readings. I included them in order to help you listen more actively for whatever it is the Lord might be saying to you.

Jesus speaks to all in the Gospels, but in your sacred reading he can now speak exclusively to you. If you can, write down what he says to you and reread his words during the day. Put all of Jesus' words to you in a folder or keep a spiritual notebook. Believers through the ages have recorded the words of Jesus to them, holy mystics and ordinary believers alike.

It takes faith to hear the voice of Jesus. This faith will grow as you practice listening. Ideally, we will learn to hear what Jesus is saying to us all day long, such as when we face difficult situations. Listening to the voice of Jesus is practicing the presence of God. As Saint Paul said, "In him we live and move and have our being" (Acts 17:28).

Saint Ignatius of Loyola called this conversation with Jesus *colloquy*. That word simply means that two or more people are talking. Saint Ignatius even urges us to include the saints in our prayer conversations. We believe in the Communion of Saints. If you have a patron saint, don't be afraid to talk to him or her. In her autobiography, Saint Thérèse of Lisieux, who was a member of the Apostleship of Prayer, describes how she spoke often with Mary and Joseph as well as with Jesus.

6. *Ask God to show you how to live today.*

Pope Benedict XVI commented that sacred reading
is not complete without a call to action: something
in our praying leads us to do something in our day.
Perhaps we find an opportunity to serve, to love, to
give, to lead, or to do something good for someone
else. Perhaps we find occasion to repent, to forgive, to
ask forgiveness, to make amends. Open your heart to
anything God might want you to do. Try to keep the
conversation with God going all day long.

Asking God to show you how to live is the last step
of the Sacred Reading prayer time, but that doesn't
mean you need to end it here. Keep it going. You may
drift off in the presence of God, lose attention, or even
fall asleep, but you can come back. God is always present, seeking to love you and to be loved. God is always
seeking to lead us to the green pastures. God is our
strength, our rock, our ever-present help in time of
trouble. God is full of mercy, ready to forgive us again
and again. God sees us through very difficult times.
God heals us. God gives his life to us constantly. God
is our Maker, Father, Mother, Lover, Servant, Savior,
and Friend. We know that from the Gospel. He is an
inexhaustible spring of blessing and holiness in our
innermost selves. The sanctification of our souls is
God's work, not our own.

As you read, ask the Holy Spirit to lead you in this
process. With genuine faith, open yourself to respond
to the Word and the Spirit, and your relationship with
Jesus will continue to deepen and to grow just as the
infant Jesus grew within the womb of the Blessed
Mother. This in turn will lead you to share the love
of Christ with all those you encounter—just as the

Blessed Mother draws all those who encounter her directly to her Son.

Other Resources to Help You

These Sacred Reading resources, including both the seasonal books and the annual prayer book, are enriched by the spirituality of the Apostleship of Prayer. Since 1844, our mission has been to encourage Catholics to pray each day for the good of the world, the Church, and the prayer intentions of the Holy Father. In particular, we encourage Christians to respond to the loving gift of Jesus Christ by making a daily offering of themselves each day. As we give the Lord our hearts, we ask him to make them like his own heart, full of love, mercy, and peace.

These booklets may be used in small groups or as a handy individual resource for those who want a special way to draw close to Christ during Advent. If you enjoy these reflections and would like to continue this prayerful reading throughout the year, pick up a copy of the *Sacred Reading* annual prayer guide. These annual books offer a personal prayer experience that can be adapted to meet your particular needs. For example, some choose to continue to reflect upon each day's reading in writing, either in the book or in a separate journal or notebook, to create a record of their spiritual journey for the entire year. Others supplement their daily reading from the book with the daily videos and other online resources available through the Apostleship of Prayer website (apostleshipofprayer.org).

If you are new to the practice of daily prayer or would like more information about a different kind of daily prayer offering, we have also included at the end of this booklet an excerpt from another Apostleship of Prayer resource, *Three Moments of the Day* by Christopher S. Collins, S.J. This book is a wonderful introduction to another form of Ignatian prayer that is central to the spirituality of the Apostleship of Prayer, the Morning Offering.

For more information about the Apostleship of Prayer and about the other resources we have developed to help men and women cultivate habits of daily prayer, visit our website at www.apostleshipofprayer.org.

I pray that this experience may help you walk closely with God every day.

> Douglas Leonard, PhD
> Executive Director
> Apostleship of Prayer

We Need Your Feedback!
Ave Maria Press and the Apostleship of Prayer would like to hear from you. After you've finished reading, please go to **avemariapress.com/feedback** to take a brief survey about your experience with *Sacred Reading for Advent and Christmas 2015–2016*. We'll use your input to make next year's book even better.

FIRST WEEK OF ADVENT

The time of Advent that we begin again today returns us to the horizon of hope, a hope that does not disappoint because it is founded on the Word of God. A hope that does not disappoint, simply because the Lord never disappoints! He is faithful!

Pope Francis
December 1, 2013

Sunday, November 29, 2015
First Sunday of Advent

Know that God is present with you and ready to converse.

We begin by taking a moment to quiet our hearts, offering back to God any distractions or cares that might cause us to miss what he wants to say.

When you are ready, invite God to speak to you with words such as these: "I seek you in your Word, my God. Jesus, you are the Word of God. You are present with me now."

Read the Gospel: Luke 21:25–28, 34–36.

Jesus said: "There will be signs in the sun, the moon, and the stars, and on the earth distress among nations confused by the roaring of the sea and the waves. People will faint from fear and foreboding of what is coming upon the world, for the powers of the heavens will be shaken. Then they will see 'the Son of Man coming in a cloud' with power and great glory. Now when these things begin to take place, stand up and raise your heads, because your redemption is drawing near. . . .

"Be on guard so that your hearts are not weighed down with dissipation and drunkenness and the worries of this life, and that day does not catch you unexpectedly, like a trap. For it will come upon all who live on the face of the whole earth. Be alert at all times, praying that you may have the strength to escape all these things that will take place and to stand before the Son of Man."

Notice what you think and feel as you read the Gospel.

This Advent begins with a reminder of Jesus' second coming, making us think about the areas of our lives that need to be put in order.

Take a moment to consider what this Gospel passage suggests to you about how you can best prepare to celebrate the Lord's coming in the Incarnation and to anticipate his return.

Pray as you are led for yourself and others.

"I am often anxious at this time of year, Lord. How does the Gospel help me prepare myself for your coming? How can I share your Incarnation with others?" (Continue in your own words.)

Listen to Jesus.

My child, I am preparing you every day. I am your strength. Put yourself in my care. Follow me into my eternal kingdom. What else is Jesus saying to you?

Ask God to show you how to live today.

As we conclude our time of prayer, we invite God to remain with us. While it is true that God is always with us, this prayer helps us to offer our day to God and to be more mindful of his presence in our daily lives.

"When I find myself anxious today, Lord, let me offer it to you and find your peace. Amen."

Linger in God's presence a few more moments.

Monday, November 30, 2015
Saint Andrew, Apostle

Know that God is present with you and ready to converse.

Take a moment to quiet your heart before you begin. "Lord, I come with my heart open to you. I need you here with me. We are together."

Read the Gospel: Matthew 4:18–22.

As Jesus walked by the Sea of Galilee, he saw two brothers, Simon, who is called Peter, and Andrew his brother, casting a net into the lake—for they were fishermen. And he said to them, "Follow me, and I will make you fish for people." Immediately they left their nets and followed him. As he went from there, he saw two other brothers, James son of Zebedee and his brother John, in the boat with their father Zebedee, mending their nets, and he called them. Immediately they left the boat and their father, and followed him.

Notice what you think and feel as you read the Gospel.

Jesus knew those he called to be his apostles. He did not interview them. They did not question him either, for the call of the Son of God was compelling. These men left jobs and family to be with him. What were they expecting?

Pray as you are led for yourself and others.

"Jesus, let me be willing to abandon all to follow you. I am in this place, doing this work. Do you want me in another place, or to do something else? How may I please you, Lord?" (Continue in your own words.)

Listen to Jesus.

Thank you for giving me time to speak with you when you pray. As I see your love for me growing in your heart, I am happy. Give yourself to me, so I can give more of myself to you. What else is Jesus saying to you?

Ask God to show you how to live today.

"Holy Spirit, show me ways to please God and to show love to others today. Amen."

Linger in God's presence a few more moments.

Tuesday, December 1, 2015

Know that God is present with you and ready to converse.

"You are here with me, Jesus. Help me as I read your Word."

Read the Gospel: Luke 10:21–24.

At that same hour Jesus rejoiced in the Holy Spirit and said, "I thank you, Father, Lord of heaven and earth, because you have hidden these things from the wise and the intelligent and have revealed them to infants; yes, Father, for such was your gracious will. All things have been handed over to me by my Father; and no one knows who the Son is except the Father, or who the Father is except the Son and anyone to whom the Son chooses to reveal him."

Then turning to the disciples, Jesus said to them privately, "Blessed are the eyes that see what you see! For I tell you that many prophets and kings desired to see what you see, but did not see it, and to hear what you hear, but did not hear it."

Notice what you think and feel as you read the Gospel.

The disciples were blessed to see Jesus, to hear and touch him. They recognized him instantly. Do we? Or are we often too self-absorbed and skeptical to see the Lord at work in our lives?

As you read this Gospel, what impression does it leave with you?

Pray as you are led for yourself and others.

"Make me like a child, Lord, so that I may recognize you in the events and people of my life. I want . . ." (Continue in your own words.)

Listen to Jesus.

If you know me, you know my Father and the Spirit. We are one. This is a mystery of love. You can find us in all the people of your life. What else is Jesus saying to you?

Ask God to show you how to live today.

"Lord, thank you for speaking to me privately, as you spoke to your disciples. Keep speaking to me, Lord. I hear you saying . . ." (Continue in conversation with Jesus awhile.)

Wednesday, December 2, 2015

Know that God is present with you and ready to converse.

"Let me be here with you now, Jesus. Let me hear what I need to hear from you today."

Read the Gospel: Matthew 15:29–37.

After Jesus had left that place, he passed along the Sea of Galilee, and he went up the mountain, where he sat down. Great crowds came to him, bringing with them the lame, the maimed, the blind, the mute, and many others. They put them at his feet, and he cured them, so that the crowd was amazed when they saw the mute speaking, the maimed whole, the lame walking, and the blind seeing. And they praised the God of Israel.

Then Jesus called his disciples to him and said, "I have compassion for the crowd, because they have been with me now for three days and have nothing to eat; and I do not want to send them away hungry, for they might faint on the way." The disciples said to him, "Where are we to get enough bread in the desert to feed so great a crowd?" Jesus asked them, "How many loaves have you?" They said, "Seven, and a few small fish." Then ordering the crowd to sit down on the ground, he took the seven loaves and the fish; and after giving thanks he broke them and gave them to the disciples, and the disciples gave them to the crowds.

And all of them ate and were filled; and they took up the broken pieces left over, seven baskets full.

Notice what you think and feel as you read the Gospel.

See how Jesus' heart goes out to the crowd. Many of them are desperate; he heals them and then feeds them. What else do you notice?

Pray as you are led for yourself and others.

"Lord, I need healing and feeding and other necessities of life. There are people I love who also need these things. Please give us . . ." (Continue in your own words.)

Listen to Jesus.

When you pray my prayer from the heart, "Give us this day our daily bread," I hear you. I give you what you need. When you pray, "Thy will be done," you are expressing your trust in me . . . What else is Jesus saying to you?

Ask God to show you how to live today.

"I give myself to you, body and soul, Lord. I am ready to receive from you what you want to give me to serve you. Make me mindful of your gifts today. Amen."

Thursday, December 3, 2015
Saint Francis Xavier, priest

**Know that God is present with
you and ready to converse.**

"I come into your presence with hope, Lord. Prepare
me to hear you."

Read the Gospel: Matthew 7:21, 24–27.

Jesus said, "Not everyone who says to me, 'Lord, Lord,'
will enter the kingdom of heaven, but only one who
does the will of my Father in heaven.

　　"Everyone then who hears these words of mine and
acts on them will be like a wise man who built his
house on rock. The rain fell, the floods came, and the
winds blew and beat on that house, but it did not fall,
because it had been founded on rock. And everyone
who hears these words of mine and does not act on
them will be like a foolish man who built his house on
sand. The rain fell, and the floods came, and the winds
blew and beat against that house, and it fell—and great
was its fall!"

**Notice what you think and feel
as you read the Gospel.**

Feel the buffeting of rain and wind on your face. On
what rock are you building your house?

Pray as you are led for yourself and others.

"How do I do the will of your Father, Jesus? Teach me
. . ." (Continue in your own words.)

Listen to Jesus.

To seek me is to find me, my child. When you give yourself to God, you are building upon the rock. Trust me to keep you safe. What else is Jesus saying to you?

Ask God to show you how to live today.

"I offer myself today, Lord, for the good of all those you have given me. Show me how to serve. Amen."

Friday, December 4, 2015

Know that God is present with you and ready to converse.

"We are here together, Lord. I praise you."

Read the Gospel: Matthew 9:27–31.

As Jesus went on from there, two blind men followed him, crying loudly, "Have mercy on us, Son of David!" When he entered the house, the blind men came to him; and Jesus said to them, "Do you believe that I am able to do this?" They said to him, "Yes, Lord." Then he touched their eyes and said, "According to your faith let it be done to you." And their eyes were opened. Then Jesus sternly ordered them, "See that no one knows of this." But they went away and spread the news about him throughout that district.

Notice what you think and feel as you read the Gospel.

Jesus heard the cry of those in need and touched them. And they could not contain their joy.

Pray as you are led for yourself and others.
"Touch me, Lord. I want to see . . ." (Continue in your own words).

Listen to Jesus.
I have given you the gift of faith in me. See your circumstances with eyes of faith, dear disciple. What else is Jesus saying to you?

Ask God to show you how to live today.
"I offer myself today, Lord, for the good of all those I encounter. Help me to play a part in opening their eyes to your love and care. Amen."

Saturday, December 5, 2015

**Know that God is present with
you and ready to converse.**
"Thank you for being here with me now, Lord."

Read the Gospel: Matthew 9:35–10:1, 5a, 7–8.
Then Jesus went about all the cities and villages, teaching in their synagogues, and proclaiming the good news of the kingdom, and curing every disease and every sickness. When he saw the crowds, he had compassion for them, because they were harassed and helpless, like sheep without a shepherd. Then he said to his disciples, "The harvest is plentiful, but the laborers are few; therefore ask the Lord of the harvest to send out laborers into his harvest."

Then Jesus summoned his twelve disciples and
gave them authority over unclean spirits, to cast them
out, and to cure every disease and every sickness. . . .
These twelve Jesus sent out with the following instruc-
tions: ". . . As you go, proclaim the good news, 'The
kingdom of heaven has come near.' Cure the sick, raise
the dead, cleanse the lepers, cast out demons. You
received without payment; give without payment."

Notice what you think and feel as you read the Gospel.

Jesus has a heart for the needy; he calls his disciples to
serve. Then he gives them power to do what is needed.
What does this say to you?

Pray as you are led for yourself and others.

"How are you calling me to serve, Jesus? What power
are you giving me to serve? I ask that . . ." (Continue
in your own words.)

Listen to Jesus.

*I need you where you are, dear one, to do what you can do.
Show love to others in every way you can. I give you power
to do that.* What else is Jesus saying to you?

Ask God to show you how to live today.

"Jesus, you gave yourself to others every day. Help me
do the same. Amen."

SECOND WEEK OF ADVENT

Advent is concerned with that very connection between memory and hope, which is so necessary to man. Advent's intention is to awaken the most profound and basic emotional memory within us, namely the memory of the God who became a child. This is a healing memory; it brings hope. The purpose of the Church's year is continually to rehearse her great history of memories, to awaken the heart's memory so that it can discern the star of hope. . . . It is the beautiful task of Advent to awaken in all of us memories of goodness and thus to open doors of hope.

Joseph Ratzinger (Pope Benedict XVI)
Seek That Which Is Above, 1986

Sunday, December 6, 2015
Second Sunday of Advent

**Know that God is present with
you and ready to converse.**

We begin by taking a moment to quiet our hearts, offering back to God any distractions or cares that might cause us to miss what he wants to say. When you are ready, invite God to speak to you with words such as these:

"Let me come into your presence with joy, Lord."

Read the Gospel: Luke 3:1–6.

In the fifteenth year of the reign of Emperor Tiberius, when Pontius Pilate was governor of Judea, and Herod was ruler of Galilee . . . the word of God came to John son of Zechariah in the wilderness. He went into all the region around the Jordan, proclaiming a baptism of repentance for the forgiveness of sins, as it is written in the book of the words of the prophet Isaiah,

"The voice of one crying out in the wilderness:
'Prepare the way of the Lord,
    make his paths straight.
Every valley shall be filled,
    and every mountain and hill shall be made
    low,
and the crooked shall be made straight,
    and the rough ways made smooth;
and all flesh shall see the salvation of God.'"

Notice what you think and feel as you read the Gospel.

John was set in motion by the Word of God, who is Jesus, to preach repentance. Repentance prepares the way of the Lord.

Take a moment to consider: How do these words of Isaiah move you?

Pray as you are led for yourself and others.

"Lord, I repent of my sins so that you can come to me. Show me the ways I resist your love, help me to forsake all habits of sin, and give me grace to . . ." (Continue in your own words.)

Listen to Jesus.

You are mine, enfolded in arms of love and peace. I forgive you and make you whole. I am strengthening you in your spirit. What else is Jesus saying to you?

Ask God to show you how to live today.

As we conclude our time of prayer, we invite God to remain with us. While it is true that God is always with us, this prayer helps us to offer our day to God, and to be more mindful of his presence in our daily lives.

"Thank you for your mercy, Jesus. How shall I become what you want me to be? What shall I do today? Amen."

Linger in God's presence a few more moments.

Monday, December 7, 2015

**Know that God is present with
you and ready to converse.**
"I welcome you into my day, Lord. Let me be with you
all day long."

Read the Gospel: Luke 5:17–26.

One day, while he was teaching, Pharisees and teachers
of the law were sitting nearby (they had come from
every village of Galilee and Judea and from Jerusalem); and the power of the Lord was with him to heal.
Just then some men came, carrying a paralyzed man
on a bed. They were trying to bring him in and lay
him before Jesus; but finding no way to bring him in
because of the crowd, they went up on the roof and let
him down with his bed through the tiles into the mid-
dle of the crowd in front of Jesus. When he saw their
faith, he said, "Friend, your sins are forgiven you."
Then the scribes and the Pharisees began to question,
"Who is this who is speaking blasphemies? Who can
forgive sins but God alone?" When Jesus perceived
their questionings, he answered them, "Why do you
raise such questions in your hearts? Which is easier, to
say, 'Your sins are forgiven you,' or to say, 'Stand up
and walk?' But so that you may know that the Son of
Man has authority on earth to forgive sins"—he said
to the one who was paralyzed—"I say to you, stand up
and take your bed and go to your home." Immediately
he stood up before them, took what he had been lying
on, and went to his home, glorifying God. Amazement
seized all of them, and they glorified God and were

filled with awe, saying, "We have seen strange things today."

Notice what you think and feel as you read the Gospel.

What an incredible scene as the friends of the paralyzed man let him down through the roof on a stretcher! Even as witnesses to his mercy and healing power, some people find fault with Jesus. What else do you see in this passage?

Pray as you are led for yourself and others.

"I, too, can find fault with my circumstances, questioning you in my heart for some trouble or some good thing I feel has been withheld from me. Give me grace to cooperate with your will, to work with you as you bring good out of all things in my life. I glorify you for . . ." (Continue in your own words.)

Listen to Jesus.

My child, I love you and I love spending this time with you. I am always near you. Look for me in your circumstances and especially in others. Do not worry about anything. What else is Jesus saying to you?

Ask God to show you how to live today.

"You deserve honor and glory, Lord. Let me worship you for your goodness. Let me know more about you, my Good Shepherd. Amen."

Tuesday, December 8, 2015
The Immaculate Conception
of the Blessed Virgin Mary

Know that God is present with you and ready to converse.

"I come to you today, Lord, seeking you. You are here now. Thank you."

Read the Gospel: Luke 1:26–38.

In the sixth month the angel Gabriel was sent by God to a town in Galilee called Nazareth, to a virgin engaged to a man whose name was Joseph, of the house of David. The virgin's name was Mary. And he came to her and said, "Greetings, favored one! The Lord is with you." But she was much perplexed by his words and pondered what sort of greeting this might be. The angel said to her, "Do not be afraid, Mary, for you have found favor with God. And now, you will conceive in your womb and bear a son, and you will name him Jesus. He will be great, and will be called the Son of the Most High, and the Lord God will give to him the throne of his ancestor David. He will reign over the house of Jacob forever, and of his kingdom there will be no end."

Mary said to the angel, "How can this be, since I am a virgin?" The angel said to her, "The Holy Spirit will come upon you, and the power of the Most High will overshadow you; therefore the child to be born will be holy; he will be called Son of God. And now, your relative Elizabeth in her old age has also conceived a son; and this is the sixth month for her who was said to be barren. For nothing will be impossible with God." Mary said, "Here am I, the servant of the Lord; let it be with me according to your word." Then the angel departed from her.

Notice what you think and feel as you read the Gospel.

Mary cannot comprehend Gabriel's stunning announcement. But she surrenders to God's will and gives her consent. She must have had many feelings about what the angel told her. What do *you* feel as you read this passage?

Pray as you are led for yourself and others.

"Hail Mary, full of grace, thank you for your willingness to give your life to the Holy Spirit so that the holy Son of God could come and redeem us. Lord Jesus, because 'nothing is impossible with God,' I ask you . . ." (Continue in your own words.)

Listen to Jesus.

I hear your prayer, my good friend. I am the One who puts love and faith in your heart. In me and through me, your prayer changes things for good. What else is Jesus saying to you?

Ask God to show you how to live today.

"I want to spend this time with you, Jesus. I have so much to learn about loving and serving you. Amen."

Wednesday, December 9, 2015

Know that God is present with you and ready to converse.

"I feel you within me and all around me, Lord. May I grow closer to you in this time of prayer."

Read the Gospel: Matthew 11:28–30.

Jesus said, "Come to me, all you that are weary and are carrying heavy burdens, and I will give you rest. Take my yoke upon you, and learn from me; for I am gentle and humble in heart, and you will find rest for your souls. For my yoke is easy, and my burden is light."

Notice what you think and feel as you read the Gospel.

Jesus invites those who are already burdened to take up his yoke. That seems surprising, until Jesus beautifully explains. What else do you hear Jesus saying?

Pray as you are led for yourself and others.

"Lord, let me learn from you. Let me take up the yoke to love God and others. Give me your own heart, gentle and lowly, that I might find rest for . . ." (Continue in your own words.)

Listen to Jesus.

Beloved, I want to speak to your heart. I know your labor and your burdens. Lay them on me. What else is Jesus saying to you?

Ask God to show you how to live today.

"How will you change my heart, Lord, to make it like your own? What shall I do today to act upon your Word? Amen."

Thursday, December 10, 2015

**Know that God is present with
you and ready to converse.**

"Give me the joy of your presence here and now, Lord. You are the Word of God."

Read the Gospel: Matthew 11:11–15.

Jesus said: "Truly I tell you, among those born of women no one has arisen greater than John the Baptist; yet the least in the kingdom of heaven is greater than he. From the days of John the Baptist until now the kingdom of heaven has suffered violence, and the violent take it by force. For all the prophets and the law prophesied until John came; and if you are willing to accept it, he is Elijah who is to come. Let anyone with ears listen!"

**Notice what you think and feel
as you read the Gospel.**

Some might find the words of Jesus here a bit puzzling. How can the least in the kingdom be greater than John? We were not there in Jesus' day. How does our faith in the Messiah differ from John's?

Pray as you are led for yourself and others.

"Jesus, give me ears to hear you calling me into the kingdom of heaven. Give me courage to follow fearlessly and with obedience . . ." (Continue in your own words.)

Listen to Jesus.

In time, I will show you the kingdom of heaven, leading you to something beyond human imagining. Know that heaven is a world of love, and you will share my glory. What else is Jesus saying to you?

Ask God to show you how to live today.

"My ears and my heart are open to you, Savior. Teach me. Amen."

Friday, December 11, 2015

Know that God is present with you and ready to converse.

"Speak to me, Lord. Your servant is with you now, listening."

Read the Gospel: Matthew 11:16–19.

Jesus said: "But to what will I compare this generation? It is like children sitting in the marketplaces and calling to one another,

'We played the flute for you, and you did not dance;
    we wailed, and you did not mourn.'

"For John came neither eating nor drinking, and they say, 'He has a demon'; the Son of Man came eating and drinking, and they say, 'Look, a glutton and a drunkard, a friend of tax collectors and sinners!' Yet wisdom is vindicated by her deeds."

Notice what you think and feel as you read the Gospel.

Jesus seems to be saying that those of his generation would respond neither to John the Baptist's stern call to repentance nor to Jesus' welcoming call to the kingdom. What about my generation? What about me?

Pray as you are led for yourself and others.

"Lord, I don't want to be a complainer. Let me respond to you with wisdom. Give me what I need to share your love with my generation." (Continue in your own words.)

Listen to Jesus.

My child, my purpose has always been your salvation—and the salvation of every person everywhere, for all of human history. I am glad you love me and want others to love me, too. Start by loving them; then you will know what to say and do. What else is Jesus saying to you?

Ask God to show you how to live today.

"Jesus, make me the person you want me to be. I give myself to you. Amen."

Saturday, December 12, 2015
Our Lady of Guadalupe

**Know that God is present with
you and ready to converse.**

"Let me be brave, Lord, and not afraid as I spend this
time with you, your Word, and your mother."

Read the Gospel: Luke 1:26–38.

In the sixth month the angel Gabriel was sent by
God to a town in Galilee called Nazareth, to a virgin
engaged to a man whose name was Joseph, of the
house of David. The virgin's name was Mary. And he
came to her and said, "Greetings, favored one! The
Lord is with you." But she was much perplexed by his
words and pondered what sort of greeting this might
be. The angel said to her, "Do not be afraid, Mary, for
you have found favor with God. And now, you will
conceive in your womb and bear a son, and you will
name him Jesus. He will be great, and will be called
the Son of the Most High, and the Lord God will give
to him the throne of his ancestor David. He will reign
over the house of Jacob forever, and of his kingdom
there will be no end."

Mary said to the angel, "How can this be, since I am
a virgin?" The angel said to her, "The Holy Spirit will
come upon you, and the power of the Most High will
overshadow you; therefore the child to be born will
be holy; he will be called Son of God. And now, your
relative Elizabeth in her old age has also conceived a

son; and this is the sixth month for her who was said to be barren. For nothing will be impossible with God."

Then Mary said, "Here am I, the servant of the Lord; let it be with me according to your word." Then the angel departed from her.

Notice what you think and feel as you read the Gospel.

Mary, the handmaid of the Lord, is also the handmaid of the Church, the Body of her son Jesus. He is the Son of the most high God who will rule over his kingdom forever.

Pray as you are led for yourself and others.

"Jesus, I honor your mother, whom you have also honored in heaven as Queen. You are a loving son to her, and as she loves you, she loves us. Mary, for love of Jesus, pray for us sinners now and at the hour of our death. . ." (Continue in your own words.)

Listen to Jesus.

I do love my mother and will honor her forever. Those who love me love her. And those who love her do the will of God and will be great in the kingdom of heaven. There is love and joy for all. What else is Jesus saying to you?

Ask God to show you how to live today.

"Lord, I delight in your promises. Your goodness overwhelms me. I am part of your family. Show me who needs my prayers today. Amen."

THIRD WEEK OF ADVENT

In the liturgy, the invitation to rejoice, to arise, resounds repeatedly, because the Lord is near, Christmas is near. Like a mother, the Church encourages us to follow faithfully the spiritual path in order to celebrate the feast of Christmas with renewed exaltation.

Pope Francis
December 15, 2013

Sunday, December 13, 2015
Third Sunday of Advent

Know that God is present with you and ready to converse.

Begin by taking a moment to quiet your heart, offering back to God any distractions or cares that might cause you to miss what he wants to say. When you are ready, invite God to speak to you with words such as these: "I am before you, my God. Teach me your ways by your Word and Spirit."

Read the Gospel: Luke 3:10–18.

And the crowds asked John the Baptist, "What then should we do?" In reply he said to them, "Whoever has two coats must share with anyone who has none; and whoever has food must do likewise." Even tax collectors came to be baptized, and they asked him, "Teacher, what should we do?" He said to them, "Collect no more than the amount prescribed for you." Soldiers also asked him, "And we, what should we do?" He said to them, "Do not extort money from anyone by threats or false accusation, and be satisfied with your wages."

As the people were filled with expectation, and all were questioning in their hearts concerning John, whether he might be the Messiah, John answered all of them by saying, "I baptize you with water; but one who is more powerful than I is coming; I am not worthy to untie the thong of his sandals. He will baptize you with the Holy Spirit and fire. His winnowing fork

is in his hand, to clear his threshing floor and to gather
the wheat into his granary; but the chaff he will burn
with unquenchable fire."

So, with many other exhortations, he proclaimed
the Good News to the people.

Notice what you think and feel as you read the Gospel.

John is a practical man, preaching generosity, justice,
and truthfulness in one's affairs. When people wonder
whether he is the Christ, John strongly opposes them.
He baptizes with water, he says; the Christ will baptize
with the Spirit and fire. Take a moment to consider
what all these images—the winnowing fork, threshing
floor, wheat, chaff, and fire—say to you.

Pray as you are led for yourself and others.

"There is something great at stake, Lord, for me and
for the whole world. Let me respond from my heart
to John's message of repentance, for I, too, have been
baptized with water. I look to you for my baptism with
the Holy Spirit." (Continue in your own words.)

Listen to Jesus.

*You may not realize what a great change I have made in your
life, dear child. The Spirit of God works in you, drawing you
to me, washing and making you holy, giving you power
to love others. Tell me what you need.* What else is Jesus
saying to you?

Ask God to show you how to live today.

Mindful of and thankful for the ways God has already changed us, we invite God to work in the moments of the day ahead. "Lord, show me today how I can serve you and others. Bring people before my mind and let me know what I can do for them that will bring glory to you. Amen."

Linger in God's presence a few more moments.

Monday, December 14, 2015

Know that God is present with you and ready to converse.

"I believe you are with me now, Savior. I seek you with my mind, my heart, and my soul."

Read the Gospel: Matthew 21:23–27.

When he entered the Temple, the chief priests and the elders of the people came to him as he was teaching and said, "By what authority are you doing these things, and who gave you this authority?" Jesus said to them, "I will also ask you one question; if you tell me the answer, then I will also tell you by what authority I do these things. Did the baptism of John come from heaven, or was it of human origin?" And they argued with one another, "If we say, 'From heaven,' he will say to us, 'Why then did you not believe him?' But if we say, 'Of human origin,' we are afraid of the crowd; for all regard John as a prophet."

So they answered Jesus, "We do not know." And he said to them, "Neither will I tell you by what authority I am doing these things."

Notice what you think and feel as you read the Gospel.

Authority is an important principle in human affairs, and it is important in godly matters as well. The chief priests and elders are trying to pin Jesus down, perhaps with genuine curiosity, but the way Jesus answers them suggests he knows they are trying to find fault. How does he turn the tables on them?

Pray as you are led for yourself and others.

"Jesus, I believe your authority is from the Father. You know all people's hearts, including mine. Let me open myself to hearing what you have to say to me today, even if it's something I may not want to hear . . ." (Continue in your own words.)

Listen to Jesus.

I love you. You are mine. I wait for you to be ready to hear what I have to say. What have I put in your heart to do for me? For someone else? What else is Jesus saying to you?

Ask God to show you how to live today.

"God, I want you to help me make plans for today and even beyond. I am your servant; show me how to serve. Amen."

Tuesday, December 15, 2015

Know that God is present with you and ready to converse.

"Jesus, you spoke even to those who opposed you when you walked the earth. You tried to instruct them. Thank you for being here now to instruct me."

Read the Gospel: Matthew 21:28–32.

Jesus said: "What do you think? A man had two sons; he went to the first and said, 'Son, go and work in the vineyard today.' He answered, 'I will not'; but later he changed his mind and went. The father went to the second and said the same; and he answered, 'I go, sir'; but he did not go. Which of the two did the will of his father?" They said, "The first." Jesus said to them, "Truly I tell you, the tax collectors and the prostitutes are going into the kingdom of God ahead of you. For John came to you in the way of righteousness and you did not believe him, but the tax collectors and the prostitutes believed him; and even after you saw it, you did not change your minds and believe him."

Notice what you think and feel as you read the Gospel.

God is far above human values and expectations. The first son is defiant, but he repents and does his father's will. The second son assents but is both disobedient and a liar.

Pray as you are led for yourself and others.

"Lord, where am I in this story? Am I more like the repentant son or the one who failed to follow through? Show me the areas of my life where I am prone to self-righteousness and hypocrisy . . ." (Continue in your own words.)

Listen to Jesus.

This is the way the human heart works—even yours, beloved friend. And yet, if you come to me, I will give you a new heart, a heart full of grace and truth, so that you can give yourself for others who need you. What else is Jesus saying to you?

Ask God to show you how to live today.

"What do I need to know and do, Lord? I want to receive your truth. Amen."

Wednesday, December 16, 2015

Know that God is present with you and ready to converse.

"You meet me here in Word and in Spirit, Lord. I love you."

Read the Gospel: Luke 7:18b–23.

So John summoned two of his disciples and sent them to the Lord to ask, "Are you the one who is to come, or are we to wait for another?" When the men had come to him, they said, "John the Baptist has sent us to you to ask, 'Are you the one who is to come, or are we to wait for another?'"

Jesus had just then cured many people of diseases, plagues, and evil spirits, and had given sight to many who were blind. And he answered them, "Go and tell John what you have seen and heard: the blind receive their sight, the lame walk, the lepers are cleansed, the deaf hear, the dead are raised, the poor have good news brought to them. And blessed is anyone who takes no offense at me."

Notice what you think and feel as you read the Gospel.

Jesus was a great wonder-worker, not for himself, but for others, especially the sick and the poor. He does not seek his own glory but lets the works speak for themselves.

Pray as you are led for yourself and others.

"Jesus, let my works also speak for themselves, that I am your friend and servant. I stumble sometimes, I sin, but I keep coming back to you for forgiveness and grace to do better. Help me to do your will . . ." (Continue in your own words.)

Listen to Jesus.

You have my grace today, my friend. Stop often to enjoy my presence with you. This is the secret of all prayer. Think about the opportunities you will have to do that today. What else is Jesus saying to you?

Ask God to show you how to live today.

"Lord, I give you all my joys and sorrows and worries.
I give you all the people that you have given to me.
How may I serve you in serving them? Amen."

Thursday, December 17, 2015

**Know that God is present with
you and ready to converse.**

"This is our time together, Lord. Let my meditation
be pleasing to you, and let me attend to your voice."

Read the Gospel: Matthew
1:1–7a, 11–13, 16–17.

An account of the genealogy of Jesus the Messiah,
the son of David, the son of Abraham. Abraham was
the father of Isaac, and Isaac the father of Jacob, and
Jacob the father of Judah and his brothers, and Judah
the father of Perez and Zerah by Tamar, and Perez the
father of Hezron, and . . . Salmon the father of Boaz by
Rahab, and Boaz the father of Obed by Ruth, and Obed
the father of Jesse, and Jesse the father of King David.

And David was the father of Solomon by the wife
of Uriah, and Solomon the father of Rehoboam, and
Rehoboam the father of Abijah, and . . . Josiah [was]
the father of Jechoniah and his brothers, at the time of
the deportation to Babylon.

And after the deportation to Babylon: Jechoniah
was the father of Salathiel, and Salathiel the father
of Zerubbabel, and . . . Jacob the father of Joseph the

husband of Mary, of whom Jesus was born, who is
called the Messiah.

So all the generations from Abraham to David are
fourteen generations; and from David to the deportation to Babylon, fourteen generations; and from
the deportation to Babylon to the Messiah, fourteen
generations.

Notice what you think and feel as you read the Gospel.

While it may be tempting to gloss over these strange
names of those in the line of Jesus, even in this
abridged version of the text, a closer look at their lives
reveals that Jesus Christ was the descendent of people
who were both good and bad. For example, the great
King Solomon was the fruit of the adulterous union
of King David and the wife of Uriah the Hittite (see
2 Sm 11:5–27). In the birth of Christ, God turned even
wicked actions to a good result. I contemplate God's
mysterious ways.

Pray as you are led for yourself and others.

"Lord, let me trust you in all my circumstances,
whether they seem good or bad. I know that you use
them all for my good and the good of others. Help me
to abandon myself completely to you . . ." (Continue
in your own words.)

Listen to Jesus.

*I came to redeem humanity. I came to save you, dear one.
Love is the sole motive behind God's mysterious ways. Trust*

in the mercy of God even in hard circumstances, such as you face now. What else is Jesus saying to you?

Ask God to show you how to live today.
"You know about my difficulties, Lord. Bring to my mind your blessings in my life. Amen."

Friday, December 18, 2015

Know that God is present with you and ready to converse.
"God, you are always with me. You are 'Emmanuel,' the God who is with us (Is 7:14) to the very end of the world (Mt 28:20)."

Read the Gospel: Matthew 1:18–25.
Now the birth of Jesus the Messiah took place in this way. When his mother Mary had been engaged to Joseph, but before they lived together, she was found to be with child from the Holy Spirit. Her husband, Joseph, being a righteous man and unwilling to expose her to public disgrace, planned to dismiss her quietly. But just when he had resolved to do this, an angel of the Lord appeared to him in a dream and said, "Joseph, son of David, do not be afraid to take Mary as your wife, for the child conceived in her is from the Holy Spirit. She will bear a son, and you are to name him Jesus, for he will save his people from their sins." All this took place to fulfill what had been spoken by the Lord through the prophet:

"Look, the virgin shall conceive and bear a son,

and they shall name him 'Emmanuel,'
which means, 'God is with us.'"

When Joseph awoke from sleep, he did as the angel
of the Lord commanded him; he took her as his wife,
but had no marital relations with her until she had
borne a son; and he named him Jesus.

Notice what you think and feel as you read the Gospel.

Joseph was a reasonable man who sought to do right
by Mary. But he must have been baffled by the situa-
tion. Through the angel in the dream, the Lord turned
Joseph completely around. He obeyed, but he still had
to wonder. What do you think Joseph was wondering?

Pray as you are led for yourself and others.

"I wonder, too, Lord, about the circumstances in my
own life. Please help me to know what you want me
to do and give me the strength to obey even if I cannot
fully understand . . ." (Continue in your own words.)

Listen to Jesus.

*My child, I do understand your circumstances. I know you
thoroughly. And I love you. You are right to give to me all
your concerns. When you do that, you will see me work in
your life.* What else is Jesus saying to you?

Ask God to show you how to live today.

"Lord, I long to see your face. How may I see you
today? Amen."

Saturday, December 19, 2015

**Know that God is present with
you and ready to converse.**

"Let me be in your presence now without fear, Lord,
for you are the Good Shepherd who is always gentle
with me."

Read the Gospel: Luke 1:5–15a; 18–25.

In the days of King Herod of Judea, there was a priest
named Zechariah, who belonged to the priestly order
of Abijah. His wife was a descendant of Aaron, and
her name was Elizabeth. Both of them were righteous
before God, living blamelessly according to all the
commandments and regulations of the Lord. But they
had no children, because Elizabeth was barren, and
both were getting on in years.

Once when he was serving as priest before God and
his section was on duty, he was chosen by lot, according to the custom of the priesthood, to enter the sanctuary of the Lord and offer incense. Now at the time of
the incense-offering, the whole assembly of the people
was praying outside. Then there appeared to him an
angel of the Lord, standing at the right side of the altar
of incense. When Zechariah saw him, he was terrified;
and fear overwhelmed him. But the angel said to him,
"Do not be afraid, Zechariah, for your prayer has been
heard. Your wife Elizabeth will bear you a son, and you
will name him John. You will have joy and gladness,
and many will rejoice at his birth, for he will be great
in the sight of the Lord. . . ."

Zechariah said to the angel, "How will I know that this is so? For I am an old man, and my wife is getting on in years." The angel replied, "I am Gabriel. I stand in the presence of God, and I have been sent to speak to you and to bring you this good news. But now, because you did not believe my words, which will be fulfilled in their time, you will become mute, unable to speak, until the day these things occur."

Meanwhile, the people were waiting for Zechariah, and wondered at his delay in the sanctuary. When he did come out, he could not speak to them, and they realized that he had seen a vision in the sanctuary. He kept motioning to them and remained unable to speak. When his time of service was ended, he went to his home.

After those days his wife Elizabeth conceived, and for five months she remained in seclusion. She said, "This is what the Lord has done for me when he looked favorably on me and took away the disgrace I have endured among my people."

Notice what you think and feel as you read the Gospel.

What might have gone through Elizabeth's mind when Zechariah returned to her, unable to speak? What does this passage suggest to you about how God answers prayer?

Pray as you are led for yourself and others.

"Almighty Lord of Hosts, heaven and earth are full of your glory. Give me eyes to see, a heart of love and

trust, and strength to do what you want me to do . . ."
(Continue in your own words.)

Listen to Jesus.

I have made you for myself, my beloved. Your prayers are like the sweetest incense to me. What else is Jesus saying to you?

Ask God to show you how to live today.

"How may I give myself quietly to you today, Lord? Amen."

FOURTH WEEK OF ADVENT

The mystery of the holy night, which historically happened two thousand years ago, must be lived as a spiritual event in the "today" of the liturgy. The Word who found a dwelling in Mary's womb comes to knock on the heart of every person with singular intensity this Christmas.

Saint John Paul II
December 19, 1999

Sunday, December 20, 2015
Fourth Sunday of Advent

Know that God is present with
you and ready to converse.

Begin by taking a moment to quiet your heart, offering back to God anything that might cause you to miss what he wants to say. When you are ready, invite God to speak to you with words such as these:

"Holy Spirit, you are here with me. Let me receive you fully into my soul while I listen to the Word of God."

Read the Gospel: Luke 1:39–45.

In those days Mary set out and went with haste to a Judean town in the hill country, where she entered the house of Zechariah and greeted Elizabeth. When Elizabeth heard Mary's greeting, the child leapt in her womb. And Elizabeth was filled with the Holy Spirit and exclaimed with a loud cry, "Blessed are you among women, and blessed is the fruit of your womb. And why has this happened to me, that the Mother of my Lord comes to me? For as soon as I heard the sound of your greeting, the child in my womb leapt for joy. And blessed is she who believed that there would be a fulfillment of what was spoken to her by the Lord."

Notice what you think and feel
as you read the Gospel.

Notice how the Holy Spirit reveals himself both through Mary, with Jesus in her womb, and through

Elizabeth, with the infant John in her womb. How does the Holy Spirit reveal his presence in your life?

Pray as you are led for yourself and others.

"Pray through me, Holy Spirit. Let me pronounce blessings upon the people in my life, particularly those in some difficulty, including . . ." (Continue in your own words.)

Listen to Jesus.

My Spirit enfolds you; you are mine. Walk in grace today and all the days of your life. Receive my peace; receive my joy. What else is Jesus saying to you?

Ask God to show you how to live today.

As our time of prayer concludes, invite God to remain with you. Although God is always with us, this prayer helps us to offer our day to God and to be more mindful of his presence.

"Who needs me today, Lord? Is there something special I can do? Amen."

Linger in God's presence a few more moments.

Monday, December 21, 2015

Know that God is present with you and ready to converse.

"You are present in your Word, Lord, and present in my heart. I am listening."

Read the Gospel: Luke 1:39–45

In those days Mary set out and went with haste to a Judean town in the hill country, where she entered the house of Zechariah and greeted Elizabeth. When Elizabeth heard Mary's greeting, the child leapt in her womb. And Elizabeth was filled with the Holy Spirit and exclaimed with a loud cry, "Blessed are you among women, and blessed is the fruit of your womb. And why has this happened to me, that the Mother of my Lord comes to me? For as soon as I heard the sound of your greeting, the child in my womb leapt for joy. And blessed is she who believed that there would be a fulfillment of what was spoken to her by the Lord."

Notice what you think and feel as you read the Gospel.

After Mary had received the startling announcement from the angel, she acted immediately. First her heart was willing to believe God, then her words consented, and then she hurried to visit her elderly cousin.

Pray as you are led for yourself and others.

"Lord, give me openness to your word like Mary's. Let me believe, say yes to you, and act in the loving ways you wish for me to act . . ." (Continue in your own words.)

Listen to Jesus.

I give you what you ask, my love. Today I give you opportunities to show your faith and to show your willingness to do God's will. Little acts of love are great acts. What else is Jesus saying to you?

Ask God to show you how to live today.
"Give me wisdom, Lord, so that I can show your love to others. Amen."

Tuesday, December 22, 2015

Know that God is present with you and ready to converse.
"You are the Almighty One, the Lord, my God, yet you are pleased to be with me now."

Read the Gospel: Luke 1:46–56.
And Mary said,

"My soul magnifies the Lord,
    and my spirit rejoices in God my Savior,
for he has looked with favor on the lowliness of his servant.
    Surely, from now on all generations will call me blessed;
for the Mighty One has done great things for me,
    and holy is his name.
His mercy is for those who fear him
    from generation to generation.
He has shown strength with his arm;
    he has scattered the proud in the thoughts of their hearts.
He has brought down the powerful from their thrones,

and lifted up the lowly;
he has filled the hungry with good things,
    and sent the rich away empty.
He has helped his servant Israel,
    in remembrance of his mercy,
according to the promise he made to our ancestors,
    to Abraham and to his descendants forever."

And Mary remained with her for about three months and then returned to her home.

Notice what you think and feel as you read the Gospel.

God opposes the proud, the mighty, and the rich. God extends blessings to those who fear God, the lowly, and the hungry. In what ways can you identify with these groups?

Pray as you are led for yourself and others.

"Lord, you know how I can be proud and self-sufficient. I do not want to be that way. Give me the blessed humility of Mary. Give me hunger for you and have mercy on me . . ." (Continue in your own words.)

Listen to Jesus.

I forgive you, child. I love to bestow mercy. Walk in it today. Who needs mercy from you? What else is Jesus saying to you?

Ask God to show you how to live today.

"My Jesus, how may I become lowly like your Blessed Mother? Amen."

Wednesday, December 23, 2015

**Know that God is present with
you and ready to converse.**

"You promised to be with me always, Lord. You are
here with me now. Mold me to your Word."

Read the Gospel: Luke 1:57–66.

Now the time came for Elizabeth to give birth, and
she bore a son. Her neighbors and relatives heard that
the Lord had shown his great mercy to her, and they
rejoiced with her.

On the eighth day they came to circumcise the child,
and they were going to name him Zechariah after his
father. But his mother said, "No; he is to be called
John." They said to her, "None of your relatives has
this name." Then they began motioning to his father to
find out what name he wanted to give him. He asked
for a writing tablet and wrote, "His name is John." And
all of them were amazed. Immediately his mouth was
opened and his tongue freed, and he began to speak,
praising God. Fear came over all their neighbors, and
all these things were talked about throughout the entire
hill country of Judea. All who heard them pondered
them and said, "What then will this child become?"
For, indeed, the hand of the Lord was with him.

Notice what you think and feel
as you read the Gospel.

The neighbors and relatives do not approve of the
name Elizabeth and Zechariah had chosen for their

son. Yet, when they obey by calling him John, the Lord confirms their choice publicly by removing Zechariah's impediment so he can speak again. Through obedience to God, we experience the greatest freedom.

Pray as you are led for yourself and others.
"Lord, the approval of neighbors and relatives is not the proper motive of my actions. I wish only to obey you. Help me to know your will and give me the strength to do it even in the face of disapproval . . ." (Continue in your own words.)

Listen to Jesus.
My beloved, I will bless you for your sincere efforts to put God first in your life. Love God and others in your thoughts, words, and actions. That is the whole will of God. What else is Jesus saying to you?

Ask God to show you how to live today.
"How shall I put you first today, Lord? Amen."

Thursday, December 24, 2015

Know that God is present with you and ready to converse.
"In the name of the Father, the Son, and the Holy Spirit, I sit with the living Word of God."

Read the Gospel: Luke 1:67–79.
Then his father Zechariah was filled with the Holy Spirit and spoke this prophecy:

"Blessed be the Lord God of Israel,
  for he has looked favorably on his people and
  redeemed them.
He has raised up a mighty savior for us
  in the house of his servant David,
as he spoke through the mouth of his holy prophets
from of old,
  that we would be saved from our enemies
  and from the hand of all who hate us.
Thus he has shown the mercy promised to our
ancestors,
  and has remembered his holy covenant,
the oath that he swore to our ancestor Abraham,
  to grant us that we, being rescued from the
  hands of our enemies,
might serve him without fear, in holiness and
righteousness
  before him all our days.
And you, child, will be called the prophet of the Most
High;
  for you will go before the Lord to prepare his
  ways,
to give knowledge of salvation to his people
  by the forgiveness of their sins.
By the tender mercy of our God,
  the dawn from on high will break upon us,
to give light to those who sit in darkness and in the
shadow of death,
  to guide our feet into the way of peace."

Notice what you think and feel as you read the Gospel.

". . . the dawn from on high will break upon us, to give light to those who sit in darkness and in the shadow of death." These beautiful words express a glorious promise. The Savior, the Christ, is coming soon.

Pray as you are led for yourself and others.

"Lord, you are great. You keep your promises. Blessed are you. Blessed are all those who trust in you. Let me be one of those . . ." (Continue in your own words.)

Listen to Jesus.

I bless you today, dear friend. Wait for me in every moment and we will walk together. What else is Jesus saying to you?

Ask God to show you how to live today.

"Lord, show me the events and people of this day as you see them. Give me your heart as I give mine to you. Amen."

THE CHRISTMAS SEASON
THROUGH EPIPHANY

O sweet Child of Bethlehem,
grant that we may share with all our hearts
in this profound mystery of Christmas.
Put into the hearts of men and women this peace
for which they sometimes seek so desperately
and which you alone can give to them.
Help them to know one another better,
and to live as brothers and sisters,
children of the same Father.
Reveal to them also your beauty, holiness, and purity.
Awaken in their hearts
love and gratitude for your infinite goodness.
Join them all together in your love.
And give us your heavenly peace. Amen.

Saint John XXIII
Journal of a Soul, 1964

Friday, December 25, 2015
The Nativity of the Lord (Christmas)

Know that God is present with
you and ready to converse.

"You have made your dwelling among us, Lord. You
have taken human flesh and blood to fulfill the pur-
poses of God."

Read the Gospel: John 1:1–18.

In the beginning was the Word, and the Word was with
God, and the Word was God. He was in the beginning
with God. All things came into being through him, and
without him not one thing came into being. What has
come into being in him was life, and the life was the
light of all people. The light shines in the darkness, and
the darkness did not overcome it.

There was a man sent from God, whose name was
John. He came as a witness to testify to the light, so
that all might believe through him. He himself was
not the light, but he came to testify to the light. The
true light, which enlightens everyone, was coming into
the world.

He was in the world, and the world came into being
through him; yet the world did not know him. He
came to what was his own, and his own people did not
accept him. But to all who received him, who believed
in his name, he gave power to become children of God,
who were born, not of blood or of the will of the flesh
or of the will of man, but of God.

And the Word became flesh and lived among us, and we have seen his glory, the glory as of a father's only son, full of grace and truth. (John testified to him and cried out, "This was he of whom I said, 'He who comes after me ranks ahead of me because he was before me.'") From his fullness we have all received grace upon grace. The law indeed was given through Moses; grace and truth came through Jesus Christ. No one has ever seen God. It is God the only Son, who is close to the Father's heart, who has made him known.

Notice what you think and feel as you read the Gospel.

The infant and the man Jesus is true God. He reveals God's glory from everlasting to everlasting, and, accepting him, we receive the power to become children of God.

Pray as you are led for yourself and others.

"Word of God, full of grace and truth, let me bathe in your light. Let me know you and love you with every atom of myself, for I was made for you. Take me and my . . ." (Continue in your own words.)

Listen to Jesus.

My child, you know I love you, teach you, and guide you on your journey. Thank you for placing yourself in my care. You may trust me. I give you my peace. What else is Jesus saying to you?

Ask God to show you how to live today.

"I am still listening, Lord. How may I please you? Amen."

Saturday, December 26, 2015
Saint Stephen, first martyr

Know that God is present with you and ready to converse.

"You were present at the death of Saint Stephen, Lord, and you are present with me now."

Read the Gospel: Matthew 10:17–22.

Jesus said: "Beware of them, for they will hand you over to councils and flog you in their synagogues; and you will be dragged before governors and kings because of me, as a testimony to them and the Gentiles. When they hand you over, do not worry about how you are to speak or what you are to say; for what you are to say will be given to you at that time; for it is not you who speak, but the Spirit of your Father speaking through you. Brother will betray brother to death, and a father his child, and children will rise against parents and have them put to death; and you will be hated by all because of my name. But the one who endures to the end will be saved."

Notice what you think and feel as you read the Gospel.

"Beware of them," Jesus says, and he goes on to describe the atrocities people will inflict, and still do inflict, upon his followers. How have you experienced these things?

Pray as you are led for yourself and others.

"Lord, Lamb of God, Prince of Peace, strengthen and comfort all who are persecuted for your sake. Give them your Spirit to speak your words and to endure to the end. I pray for peace and love in my family . . ." (Continue in your own words.)

Listen to Jesus.

Be at peace, dear friend, for I am bringing good out of each act of hatred and violence. Trust me. Give my peace to each person you encounter, especially anyone who hates you. What else is Jesus saying to you?

Ask God to show you how to live today.

"Holy Spirit, give me the words to say when I am persecuted, abused, scorned, or neglected. Amen."

Sunday, December 27, 2015
The Holy Family of Jesus,
Mary, and Joseph

Know that God is present with you and ready to converse.

Begin the week by placing yourself deliberately in God's presence. Take a moment to offer to him any distractions or cares that might cause you to miss what he wants to tell you. Acknowledge the gift of his presence: "I know you are present, around me and within me now. I depend on that, my God."

Read the Gospel: Luke 2:41–52.

Now every year Jesus' parents went to Jerusalem for the festival of the Passover. And when he was twelve years old, they went up as usual for the festival. When the festival was ended and they started to return, the boy Jesus stayed behind in Jerusalem, but his parents did not know it. Assuming that he was in the group of travelers, they went a day's journey. Then they started to look for him among their relatives and friends. When they did not find him, they returned to Jerusalem to search for him.

After three days they found him in the Temple, sitting among the teachers, listening to them and asking them questions. And all who heard him were amazed at his understanding and his answers. When his parents saw him they were astonished; and his mother said to him, "Child, why have you treated us like this? Look, your father and I have been searching for you in great anxiety." He said to them, "Why were you searching for me? Did you not know that I must be in my Father's house?" But they did not understand what he said to them. Then he went down with them and came to Nazareth, and was obedient to them. His mother treasured all these things in her heart.

And Jesus increased in wisdom and in years, and in divine and human favor.

Notice what you think and feel as you read the Gospel.

Imagine how anxiously Mary and Joseph must have looked for their boy, Jesus. Jesus' behavior is a reminder that he was a boy like other boys, just as he was to become a man like other men. Yet he was always uniquely aware of his relationship to his Father.

Pray as you are led for yourself and others.

"Jesus, through you I also have a relationship with the heavenly Father. Let me love God more truly, more deeply, more completely than I ever have. I want to pray for these children today . . ." (Continue in your own words.)

Listen to Jesus.

You and I are truly children of my Father, Creator of heaven and earth, all things and all people. Rejoice in that. Know that you can trust God to care for you as long as you live. What else is Jesus saying to you?

Ask God to show you how to live today.

As you conclude this time of prayer, invite God to remain with you and to make you more mindful of his presence throughout the day.

"What will heaven be, Lord? How may I prepare for my service to you? Amen."

Linger in his presence a few moments longer.

Monday, December 28, 2015
The Holy Innocents, martyrs

Know that God is present with you and ready to converse.

"You are with me here every day in joy or in sorrow. Thank you for that."

Read the Gospel: Matthew 2:13–18.

Now after they had left, an angel of the Lord appeared to Joseph in a dream and said, "Get up, take the child and his mother, and flee to Egypt, and remain there until I tell you; for Herod is about to search for the child, to destroy him." Then Joseph got up, took the child and his mother by night, and went to Egypt, and remained there until the death of Herod. This was to fulfill what had been spoken by the Lord through the prophet, "Out of Egypt I have called my son."

When Herod saw that he had been tricked by the wise men, he was infuriated, and he sent and killed all the children in and around Bethlehem who were two years old or under, according to the time that he had learned from the wise men. Then was fulfilled what had been spoken through the prophet Jeremiah:

"A voice was heard in Ramah,
    wailing and loud lamentation,
Rachel weeping for her children;
    she refused to be consoled, because they are
    no more."

Notice what you think and feel as you read the Gospel.

The mysterious juxtaposition of God's power and man's free will is seen clearly in this passage. Wicked Herod massacres all those babies and toddlers, as Jeremiah prophesied; yet God protects the Holy Family.

Pray as you are led for yourself and others.

"I am at a loss to understand you in this Gospel, God. Many terrible things happen in this world. Help me to know what I should do. Help me to trust you in all things . . ." (Continue in your own words.)

Listen to Jesus.

I want you to trust in God in all things. I know this is sometimes difficult. I, too, have felt afraid and forsaken. In hard times, give yourself entirely to God. God will see you through. What else is Jesus saying to you?

Ask God to show you how to live today.

"Lord, show me what my response should be to violent and frightening world events. Amen."

Tuesday, December 29, 2015

Know that God is present with
you and ready to converse.

"Open me to your nearness, Lord. Open my heart to
your Word."

Read the Gospel: Luke 2:22–35.

When the time came for their purification according to
the law of Moses, Mary and Joseph brought Jesus up
to Jerusalem to present him to the Lord (as it is written
in the law of the Lord, "Every firstborn male shall be
designated as holy to the Lord"), and they offered a
sacrifice according to what is stated in the law of the
Lord, "a pair of turtle doves or two young pigeons."

Now there was a man in Jerusalem whose name
was Simeon; this man was righteous and devout, looking forward to the consolation of Israel, and the Holy
Spirit rested on him. It had been revealed to him by the
Holy Spirit that he would not see death before he had
seen the Lord's Messiah. Guided by the Spirit, Simeon
came into the Temple; and when the parents brought
in the child Jesus, to do for him what was custom-
ary under the law, Simeon took him in his arms and
praised God, saying,

"Master, now you are dismissing your servant in
peace,
    according to your word;
for my eyes have seen your salvation,
    which you have prepared in the presence of
    all peoples,

a light for revelation to the Gentiles
and for glory to your people Israel."

And the child's father and mother were amazed at
what was being said about him. Then Simeon blessed
them and said to his mother, Mary, "This child is destined for the falling and the rising of many in Israel,
and to be a sign that will be opposed so that the inner
thoughts of many will be revealed—and a sword will
pierce your own soul, too."

Notice what you think and feel as you read the Gospel.

Simeon prophesizes that Jesus is destined to be a sign
to be contradicted, opposed, and pierced. (Even his
mother will be pierced.) What do you think it means
that through their suffering "the inner thoughts of
many will be revealed"?

Pray as you are led for yourself and others.

"Lord, you suffered and died at the hands of your
tormenters. Your side was pierced, and blood and
water gushed out for the salvation of the world. Let
the hearts of many embrace you, for you are the light
for the Gentiles and glory for your people Israel . . ."
(Continue in your own words.)

Listen to Jesus.

*I died a violent death to bring salvation, life, and peace to all
who come to me. You have come to me, my beloved. Be my
own.* What else is Jesus saying to you?

Ask God to show you how to live today.

"How may I give myself to you today, Lord? Amen."

Wednesday, December 30, 2015

**Know that God is present with
you and ready to converse.**

"Like the prophetess Anna, let me recognize your presence with me now, Lord, and give you thanks."

Read the Gospel: Luke 2:36–40.

There was also a prophet, Anna the daughter of Phanuel, of the tribe of Asher. She was of a great age, having lived with her husband for seven years after her marriage, then as a widow to the age of eighty-four. She never left the Temple but worshiped there with fasting and prayer night and day. At that moment she came and began to praise God and to speak about the child to all who were looking for the redemption of Jerusalem.

When they had finished everything required by the law of the Lord, they returned to Galilee, to their own town of Nazareth. The child grew and became strong, filled with wisdom; and the favor of God was upon him.

**Notice what you think and feel
as you read the Gospel.**

What marvelous things happened in the life of the Holy Family! The hearts of Mary and Joseph must have been filled with joy and amazement. They watched

Jesus grow and become strong, full of wisdom and the favor of God.

Pray as you are led for yourself and others.
"Jesus, I am a child, too. I await my own redemption and the redemption of the many I love. I thank you that I am growing in God's wisdom and favor . . ." (Continue in your own words.)

Listen to Jesus.
Grow in God's wisdom, child. It's not complicated. The secret is simply to give yourself to me and to those I give to you. What else is Jesus saying to you?

Ask God to show you how to live today.
"Show me how to walk in your way today, Lord. Amen."

Thursday, December 31, 2015

Know that God is present with you and ready to converse.
"I belong to you, Lord, not to the world. I know you are with me."

Read the Gospel: John 1:1–18.
In the beginning was the Word, and the Word was with God, and the Word was God. He was in the beginning with God. All things came into being through him, and without him not one thing came into being. What has come into being in him was life, and the life was the

light of all people. The light shines in the darkness, and the darkness did not overcome it.

There was a man sent from God, whose name was John. He came as a witness to testify to the light, so that all might believe through him. He himself was not the light, but he came to testify to the light. The true light, which enlightens everyone, was coming into the world.

He was in the world, and the world came into being through him; yet the world did not know him. He came to what was his own, and his own people did not accept him. But to all who received him, who believed in his name, he gave power to become children of God, who were born, not of blood or of the will of the flesh or of the will of man, but of God.

And the Word became flesh and lived among us, and we have seen his glory, the glory as of a father's only son, full of grace and truth. (John testified to him and cried out, "This was he of whom I said, 'He who comes after me ranks ahead of me because he was before me.'") From his fullness we have all received grace upon grace. The law indeed was given through Moses; grace and truth came through Jesus Christ. No one has ever seen God. It is God the only Son, who is close to the Father's heart, who has made him known.

Notice what you think and feel as you read the Gospel.

There is no beginning with God. Before the beginning, God already was, with Jesus, the eternal Word of God. Through him, with him, and in him all things were made, and all things exist.

Pray as you are led for yourself and others.

"I give you glory, Word of the Father. Thank you for shedding your true light on me. May darkness never overcome it."(Continue in your own words.)

Listen to Jesus.

I am close to you now. Our words come together in holy conversation. I am listening to you. What else is Jesus saying to you?

Ask God to show you how to live today.

"Plant your words in me, Lord, and let them grow for the good of others. Amen." Remain with Jesus awhile.

Friday, January 1, 2016
Mary, Mother of God

Know that God is present with you and ready to converse.

"I come into your presence with gladness, Lord."

Read the Gospel: Luke 2:16–21.

So the shepherds went with haste and found Mary and Joseph, and the child lying in the manger. When they saw this, they made known what had been told them about this child; and all who heard it were amazed at what the shepherds told them. But Mary treasured all these words and pondered them in her heart. The shepherds returned, glorifying and praising God for all they had heard and seen, as it had been told them.

After eight days had passed, it was time to circumcise the child; and he was called Jesus, the name given by the angel before he was conceived in the womb.

Notice what you think and feel as you read the Gospel.

Simple shepherds are among those privileged to see the infant Jesus; God must have been pleased by their hearts. Mary keeps these wonderful events in her motherly heart.

Pray as you are led for yourself and others.

"Like the shepherds, I offer you my simple thanks, Lord. I thank you and praise you for coming among us for the salvation of people, myself included. Let me be a sign to others of your great goodness . . ." (Continue in your own words.)

Listen to Jesus.

You are mine. It makes me happy when you approach me with love and thanksgiving. Beloved friend, I give your life meaning; live every day for love. What else is Jesus saying to you?

Ask God to show you how to live today.

"God, let me treasure your blessings in my heart, just as Mary did. Amen."

Saturday, January 2, 2016

**Know that God is present with
you and ready to converse.**

"Stir up my heart and mind, Lord, to hear and obey
your Word."

Read the Gospel: John 1:19–28.

This is the testimony given by John when the Jews sent
priests and Levites from Jerusalem to ask him, "Who
are you?" He confessed and did not deny it, but confessed, "I am not the Messiah."

And they asked him, "What then? Are you Elijah?"
He said, "I am not."

"Are you the prophet?" He answered, "No."

Then they said to him, "Who are you? Let us have
an answer for those who sent us. What do you say
about yourself?" He said,

"I am the voice of one crying out in the wilderness,
  'Make straight the way of the Lord,'

as the prophet Isaiah said."

Now they had been sent from the Pharisees. They
asked him, "Why then are you baptizing if you are
neither the Messiah, nor Elijah, nor the prophet?"

John answered them, "I baptize with water. Among
you stands One whom you do not know, the One who
is coming after me; I am not worthy to untie the thong
of his sandal." This took place in Bethany across the
Jordan where John was baptizing.

**Notice what you think and feel
as you read the Gospel.**

John freely admits he is not the Messiah. He says he is not worthy to untie the sandal of the One who will come after him. How did they likely respond to this?

Pray as you are led for yourself and others.

"Thank you for my baptism by water, Lord. I repent of all my sins and ask for your grace to resist sin today . . ." (Continue in your own words.)

Listen to Jesus.

I give you my forgiveness and my grace as you have prayed. In this way, you are making our way straight, for I want to be with you and walk with you today in love. What else is Jesus saying to you?

Ask God to show you how to live today.

"Lord, some days I feel unworthy of you, but I'm so grateful for your loving presence and your constant grace. Let's walk together today. Amen."

Sunday, January 3, 2016
Epiphany of the Lord

**Know that God is present with
you and ready to converse.**

On this final day of the Christmas season, pause to put yourself in the presence of the Lord, just like the magi.

"Wise men seek you and find you, Lord, right here, in this moment."

Read the Gospel: Matthew 2:1–12.

In the time of King Herod, after Jesus was born in Bethlehem of Judea, wise men from the East came to Jerusalem, asking, "Where is the child who has been born king of the Jews? For we observed his star at its rising, and have come to pay him homage." When King Herod heard this, he was frightened, and all Jerusalem with him; and calling together all the chief priests and scribes of the people, he inquired of them where the Messiah was to be born. They told him, "In Bethlehem of Judea; for so it has been written by the prophet:

'And you, Bethlehem, in the land of Judah,
    are by no means least among the rulers of
    Judah;
for from you shall come a ruler
    who is to shepherd my people Israel.'"

Then Herod secretly called for the wise men and learned from them the exact time when the star had appeared. Then he sent them to Bethlehem, saying, "Go and search diligently for the child; and when you have found him, bring me word so that I may also go and pay him homage." When they had heard the king, they set out; and there, ahead of them, went the star that they had seen at its rising, until it stopped over the place where the child was. When they saw that the star had stopped, they were overwhelmed with joy. On entering the house, they saw the child with Mary his mother; and they knelt down and paid him homage.

Then, opening their treasure chests, they offered him gifts of gold, frankincense, and myrrh. And having been warned in a dream not to return to Herod, they left for their own country by another road.

Notice what you think and feel as you read the Gospel.

I marvel that God led these mysterious and exotic wise men, magi from the east, to Bethlehem to honor the newborn king. They are overjoyed. What did they know about what they were seeing?

Pray as you are led for yourself and others.

"Lord, I seek you, too. I give you the gift of myself today. Use me as you will. That will be a joy to me . . ." (Continue in your own words.)

Listen to Jesus.

I am always with you, my dear one. We have found one another, for I also seek you. Look for me in everything, especially in the faces of those in need. What else is Jesus saying to you?

Ask God to show you how to live today.

"Show me yourself all along the way, Lord. Give me eyes for only you. Amen."

Please Take Our Survey!
Now that you've finished reading *Sacred Reading for Advent and Christmas 2015–2016*, please go to **avemariapress.com/feedback** to take a brief survey about your experience. Ave Maria Press and the Apostleship of Prayer appreciate your feedback.

A SPECIAL GIFT FOR YOU

An Excerpt from *Three Moments of the Day: Praying with the Heart of Jesus* by Christopher S. Collins, S.J.

When I look at the image of the Sacred Heart, I see at once the image of God who has assumed a heart of flesh (Incarnation) that is wounded and bloodied (paschal mystery) and at the same time aflame with an unquenchable fire of love (Resurrection). And if this Heart signifies who Christ is, then it also points to who I am called to be. I can find my true self in living according to this vision.

My daily prayer, then, should lead me to live in this way: opened to the world, vulnerable, and simultaneously pierced and burning with love. If I can do this, I need never lose hope, for I will have accomplished God's ultimate vision, the purpose for which I was created.

So, how can I pray in such a way that disposes me to become more and more like this—united to the Heart of Christ?

Rediscover the Daily Prayer of the Heart

Over time, some Jesuit friends and I adopted a method of prayer that we later discovered had been established long before we took up the practice. This approach involves offering my heart and my life to God at three separate "moments" of each day.

At the beginning of the day, I say to Jesus, "I want to live this day, and all that's in it, not in isolation but with you. I want to offer what's in my heart to what's in your Heart."

At the end of the day, I take another moment to look back and see how it's gone. This prayer, or Examen, is based on one of the ways of praying taught by St. Ignatius of Loyola in his *Spiritual Exercises*. This is a simple act of using the memory to pay attention to what actually happened in the day. Little by little, I developed a habit of speaking to Jesus about all that is ordinary in my life. As I continued this daily practice of engaging in brief exchanges every morning and evening, it began to change how I looked at the world.

The third "moment" covers the spiritual reality of the whole day. We might think of this moment as a continuation of the celebration of the Eucharist, the source and summit of our lives. Whether or not we attended Mass on a particular day, the ordinariness of everyday life is best understood in light of this "moment" of prayer in which the whole Church engages all over the world, every day. Although you and I cannot be physically present at every moment and in every place this prayer is being offered, we are part of this mystery. What goes on in the Eucharist gives a framework for understanding and making choices in daily life that will lead me out of isolation and into relationship, into dialogue, and into friendship with God. . . .

As you start praying like this, little by little, you will get in the habit of speaking to Jesus about all that is ordinary in your life. Then you'll begin to realize that by speaking about it to him, things are starting to change—or you are changing. Everything is changing. Things might not have gotten fixed the way you asked or expected, but they did get fixed. These brief exchanges of speaking and listening during the day will change the landscapes of your life. This prayer practice can change how you see the world.

To order a copy of this book, contact the Apostleship of Prayer (apostleshipofprayer.org) or Ave Maria Press (avemariapress.com).

The Apostleship of Prayer is an international Jesuit prayer ministry that reaches more than 50 million members worldwide through its popular website, *ApostleshipofPrayer.org*, and through talks, conferences, publications, and retreats such as Hearts on Fire. Known as "the pope's prayer group," the Apostleship's mission is to encourage Christians to make a daily offering of themselves to the Lord; at its center is the love of the Sacred Heart of Jesus. Douglas Leonard has served as executive director of the Apostleship of Prayer in the United States since 2006.

The
SACRED
READING
Series

Inspired by the traditions of Ignatian spirituality, the Sacred Reading series by the Apostleship of Prayer—an international Jesuit prayer ministry—is a unique guide to the use of lectio divinia through a simple, six-step process that provides a prayerful and imaginative exploration of the daily gospel readings and helps readers look for application in their own lives.

Ignatian Spirituality for Every Season

Find next year's editions wherever books and eBooks are sold.
For more information, **visit avemariapress.com.**

AVE MARIA PRESS
A Ministry of the United States
Province of Holy Cross